ANIMAL LIVES
SHARKS

Sally Morgan

QEB Publishing

The words in **bold** are
explained in the
Glossary on page 31.

Photo credits

Key: t = top, b = bottom, m = middle,
c = center, l = left, r = right

Ecoscene: 5b Phillip Colla, 5t Phillip Colla, 6l V&W Kelvin Aitken, 6-7 /Reinhard Dirsherl, 7 Matt9122,
12 V&W Brandon Cole, 15tr John Lewis, 16b V&W Kelvin Aitken, 18bl Phillip Colla, 25 Phillip Colla

FLPA: 10l Jack Perks/FLPA, 10-11 Brandelet, 11r stephan kerkhofs, 30t Jack Perks/FLPA

Getty Images: 13 Jeff Rotman, 18 Gerard Soury, 27t Chuck Davis, 30l Steven Trainoff Ph.D.

Seapics.com: 23tr © Peter Parks

Shutterstock: 2-3 Dray van Beeck, 4-5 Stubblefield Photography, 8-9 Rich Carey, 14-15 Joost van Uffelen,
16-17 cbpix, 18-19 A Cotton Photo, 20 MP cz, 21t Alexius Sutandio, 21b BW Folsom, 22-23 kaschibo, 24l
amidala76, 26-27 Tony Hunt, 28-29 Ian Scott, 29b Natali Glado, 30b Boris Pamikov, 30-31 Brandelet,
32 Ethan Daniels, 32b FAUP

Contents

The shark

Sharks are some of the most amazing creatures in the ocean. Although they are a type of fish, sharks are also vertebrates, which means that they have a backbone. On the top of their backs sharks have a large, triangle-shaped fin that sticks up out of the water when they swim near the surface. They have two large **pectoral fins**, one on each side of their body, behind the **gill slits**. They have other fins, too.

FANTASTIC FACT

The biggest ever great white shark was 23 feet (7 meters) long and weighed about 7,050 pounds (3,200 kilograms).

This blue shark has five gill slits on each side of its head.

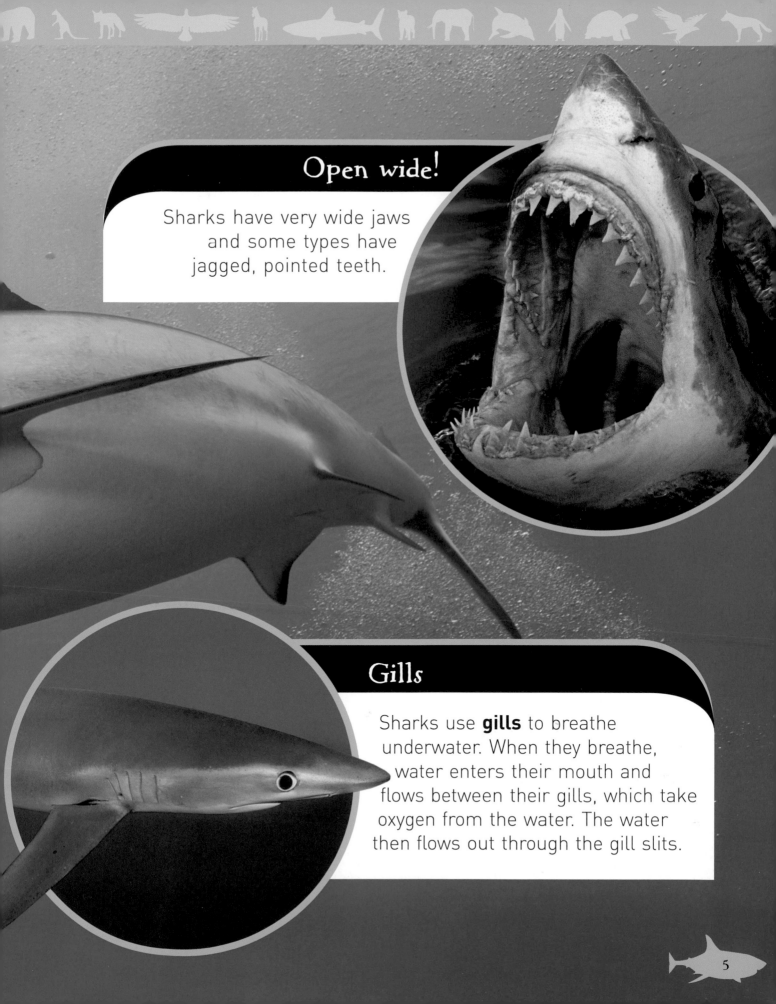

Open wide!

Sharks have very wide jaws and some types have jagged, pointed teeth.

Gills

Sharks use **gills** to breathe underwater. When they breathe, water enters their mouth and flows between their gills, which take oxygen from the water. The water then flows out through the gill slits.

Shark types

With more than 360 different **species**, divided into 30 separate families, sharks range incredibly in size, from as small as a person's hand to bigger than a bus. Surprisingly, more than half of all sharks are less than 3 feet (1 meter) long. The largest sharks, such as the whale shark and the hammerhead shark, are found far out in the open seas and oceans.

Carpet shark

The carpet shark uses **camouflage** to blend in with the seabed.

Zebra shark

Zebra sharks are slender and covered in brown spots. They grow to nearly 10 feet (3 meters) long.

Rare and common sharks

Some types of shark are very rare, such as the megamouth. The dogfish shark and the bull shark are far more common.

Tiger shark

Tiger sharks are large and can measure up to 20 feet (6 meters) long. They are found in warm seas.

FANTASTIC FACTS

The largest shark is the whale shark at up to 50 feet (15 meters) long, while the smallest are the dwarf lanternshark and the spined pygmy shark, which both grow to 7 inches (18 centimeters) long.

Where sharks live

Sharks are found in all the oceans of the world, apart from the coldest waters of the Arctic and Antarctic. Although some sharks remain in the same region for their entire lives, others swim from ocean to ocean.

Where do sharks live?

Many sharks live their whole lives in the open ocean, thousands of miles from land. Some of the smallest sharks, such as the dogfish, can be found in shallow waters at the beach.

Some sharks live in warm coastal and offshore waters.

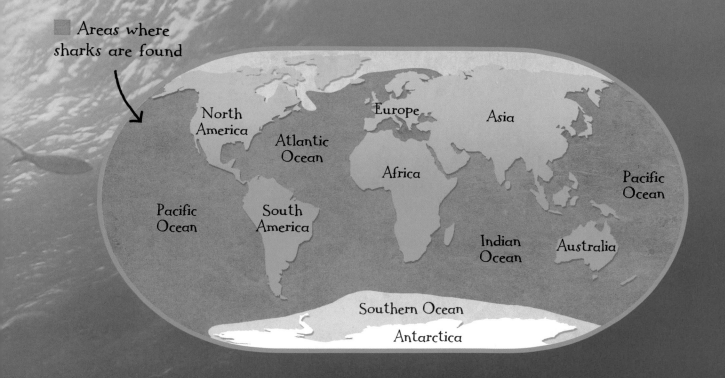

Areas where sharks are found

North America

Europe

Asia

Atlantic Ocean

Africa

Pacific Ocean

Pacific Ocean

South America

Indian Ocean

Australia

Southern Ocean

Antarctica

Living in the ocean

Some sharks stay close to the ocean floor, for example wobbegongs and angel sharks. Both types of shark have flattened bodies that are well camouflaged, which means they can hide unseen on the seabed. Other sharks live deep in the ocean, hiding in the dark water during the day and feeding at the surface at night.

FANTASTIC FACT

The bull shark swims up large rivers such as the Amazon, and can be found hundreds of miles from the ocean.

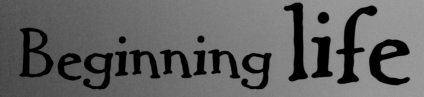

Beginning life

After mating, most female sharks produce only a few large-sized eggs. Most sharks keep their eggs safely inside their body until they are ready to give birth to live young. But some sharks lay their eggs outside their body, and each egg is protected by a tough case. Inside the case there is a large yolk that supplies food for the baby shark until it is ready to **hatch**.

Shark eggs

The dogfish shark's egg attaches itself to rocks or seaweed so that it does not float off into deep water.

Hammerhead sharks gather in large shoals during the breeding season.

Baby sharks

Baby sharks are called pups and look like miniature adult sharks. They even have a full set of teeth so as soon as they are born, they can take care of themselves.

FANTASTIC FACT

The great white shark gives birth to only one or two pups, but blue and whale sharks can have more than 100 during a single birth!

Growing up

As soon as shark pups are born they swim away from their mother. It is important that they leave the parent very quickly because some female sharks eat their own pups. Sharks grow slowly and may take many years to become a full-sized adult. They then continue to grow throughout their life.

The scars on this great white shark suggest he's very old.

How long do sharks live?

Nobody is sure how long sharks live. Most of them probably live for less than 25 years, but a few types of shark have been known to live for much longer. Some of the larger species of female shark are not ready to breed until the female is between 6 and 18 years old. Most females produce eggs every two years.

FANTASTIC FACT

Sharks are very hard to track and so it is very difficult to know the age of sharks or how long they live.

Pups

Shark pups rarely see either of their parents again, so they are independent from birth.

Swimming

The majority of sharks must keep swimming in order to breathe. Some species push themselves through the water using the force of their powerful tails while others thrust their bodies from side to side to propel themselves through the water. Some sharks are able to keep breathing while stationary by pumping water across their gills.

FANTASTIC FACT

Some of the fast sharks can cut through the water at speeds of up to 40 miles (65 kilometers) per hour.

Large pectoral fins behind the gill slits help with balance.

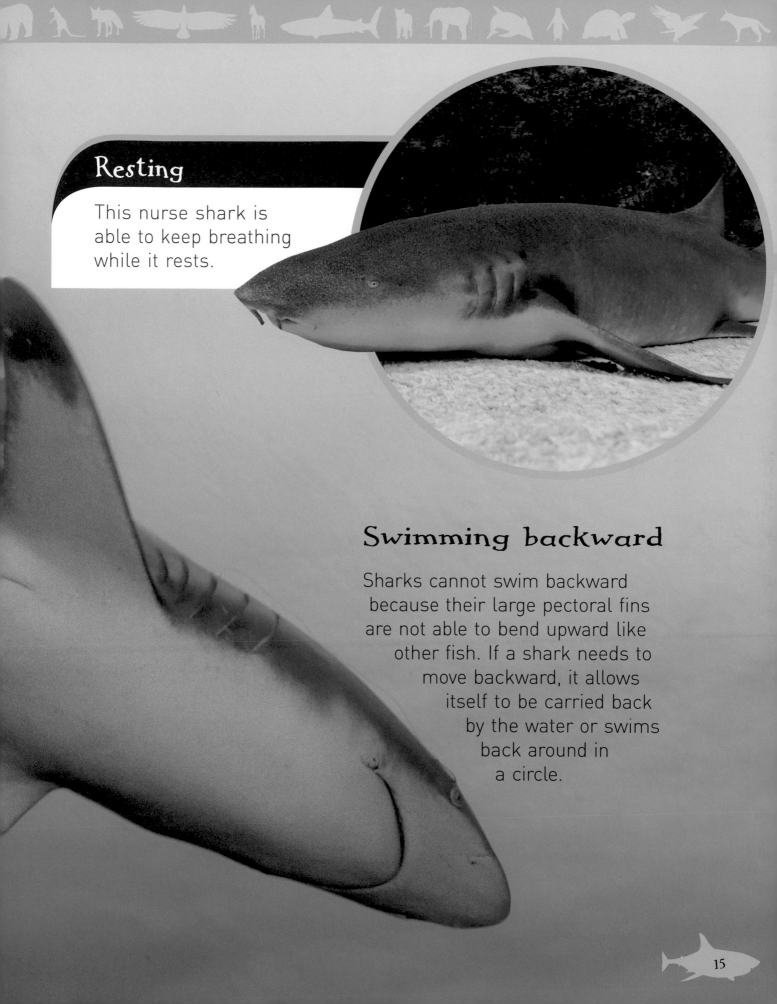

Resting

This nurse shark is able to keep breathing while it rests.

Swimming backward

Sharks cannot swim backward because their large pectoral fins are not able to bend upward like other fish. If a shark needs to move backward, it allows itself to be carried back by the water or swims back around in a circle.

Predators

Sharks are **predators**. This means that they hunt and eat other animals in order to survive. Although sharks eat a variety of foods, their diet is mainly made up of fish and **invertebrates**, such as squid and octopus. The larger sharks can catch bigger **prey**, including turtles, seals, and even dolphins. Other sharks eat animals that live on the seabed, such as crabs, starfish, sea urchins, and sea anemones.

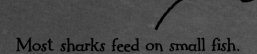

Most sharks feed on small fish.

Dinner time!

A horn shark enjoys a meal of squid eggs on the sea floor.

What do sharks eat?

A hungry shark is not very fussy about its food. In fact it will eat almost anything it finds, including any dead animals that it finds floating in the ocean. Tiger sharks are possibly the least picky of the species and eat the most varied diet. Not only do they catch live animals, such as fish and seals, but they will even feed on garbage!

FANTASTIC FACT

An unusual variety of objects have been found in sharks' stomachs, including parts of cows, dogs, penguins, wristwatches, tin cans—even shoes!

Hunting

Sharks hunt in different ways and many attack their prey from below. The hungry shark lurks in the deep water where it cannot be seen. Then, when it spots its prey, the shark races after it at great speed, charging upward out of the darkness of the deep. When hunting, the thresher shark takes full advantage of its long, sturdy tail. Once it spots a shoal of fish, it uses its tail to herd the fish together. Next it stuns them with powerful slaps, again using its mighty tail.

Lurking

Some sharks lie in wait for their prey.

Hunting groups

Although most sharks hunt alone, a few species hunt in packs. Groups of sand tiger sharks, for example, herd shoals of fish into shallow water where they can attack them more easily. Shark pups have to learn to hunt on their own, and many die before they are fully grown.

Hunting in groups helps sharks to catch prey.

FANTASTIC FACT

After eating a large meal weighing 75 pounds (35 kilograms), a great white shark will not need to eat for another 45 days.

Shark teeth

A shark's teeth can be big or small, sharp or blunt, jagged or smooth. The shape of its teeth will have **adapted** to the type of food it eats. Flat teeth are suitable for crunching snails, crabs, and sea urchins, while jagged teeth are ideal for chewing larger animals. A shark's jaws are only loosely connected to its skull, so it can open its mouth extremely wide to swallow large prey.

Big teeth!

As sharks get older, their teeth get larger, so the oldest sharks have the largest teeth.

FANTASTIC FACT

The great white shark has about 300 teeth in its huge mouth.

The tooth of a great white shark

Replacing teeth

Shark pups are born with a full set of teeth already in place. They are the same as adult teeth, but smaller. All sharks have several rows of teeth, but most use only their front row when feeding. The other rows are replacement teeth, to use when the original teeth wear away or fall out. Some types of shark use as many as 30,000 teeth during their lifetime.

Plankton eaters

The whale shark is not only the largest shark in the world, it is also the world's biggest fish. Both the whale shark and the basking shark are **filter feeders**, so they eat the tiny plants and animals, called **plankton**, that float in the water.

A whale shark is about 45 feet (13 meters) long and makes the diver swimming beside it look tiny.

Big whale, tiny teeth

Whale sharks have 300 tiny teeth in their mouth but it's unclear what they are used for.

Eating without teeth

Filter-feeding sharks may have teeth, but they don't use them. They feed by swimming steadily forward with their huge mouths wide open, scooping up water and plankton as they go. The sea water flows through their gills where it is filtered. Then the shark eats the food that is trapped.

FANTASTIC FACT

When a basking shark is feeding, nearly 2000 tons of water pass through its gills every hour.

Shark senses

Sharks use their senses to detect prey, especially their senses of smell and sight. Sharks can detect blood in the water from a distance of a mile or two. They can even pick up the sounds and **vibrations** of animals moving in the water hundreds of yards away. As they get closer to their prey, sharks use their eyes to find it.

On the prowl

Sharks like this sand tiger shark make use of all their senses when they are tracking prey.

Hammerhead

The hammerhead shark has a very oddly shaped head. Its eyes are nearly 3 feet (1 metre) apart!

Sensing movement

The front of a shark's head is called a snout. It is a little like the human nose. The **ampullae of Lorenzini** on the shark's snout are highly sensitive and can detect the electric signals that are produced when other animals move their muscles. This sense means that a shark can detect animals in the water, even if they are hidden.

FANTASTIC FACT

Some sharks may be able to track their prey by smell from up to a mile away, by following a trail of tiny particles of blood.

Sharks and people

Many people are scared of being attacked by sharks when they are in the water, but most sharks are harmless. Only about forty species have been known to attack humans. The world's four most dangerous sharks are the great white, tiger, bull, and white-tipped reef sharks.

Scary sharks

Many people fear great white sharks. However, tiger sharks are more dangerous.

Shark attacks

Occasionally sharks attack humans because they mistake them for other animals. If an injured person in the water was bleeding, for example, a shark would be attracted by the scent of the blood. In parts of the world where shark attacks have taken place, such as Australia and South Africa, many beaches are protected by shark nets.

FANTASTIC FACT

Each year there are between 70 and 100 shark attacks in the world. Only about five to ten are fatal.

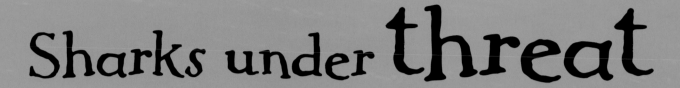

Sharks under threat

Many sharks are killed for their fins, which are used to make shark fin soup. Large sharks breed slowly and, if they are **overfished**, their numbers quickly fall. The United States and the European Union have banned **shark finning** to protect the shark population. In some places sharks are threatened because there is too much fishing in general, and not enough food left for the sharks to eat.

FANTASTIC FACT

As many as 100 million sharks are caught and killed each year—many of them for their fins.

Don't be scared of sharks!

Many people are afraid of sharks, but these amazing animals are an important part of the ocean system. Shark tourism encourages people to get to know sharks better. On some coral reefs, food is left out to attract sharks so divers can get close to them. Shark tourism earns money for local people and means that the sharks are less likely to be killed.

On organized trips, divers can swim with sharks.

Shark fin soup

Only the fins are needed for shark fin soup. Often the rest of the shark's body is simply thrown back into the sea.

Life cycle of a shark

Female sharks produce eggs. Some sharks lay their eggs in the water, while others give birth to live young. The eggs hatch into tiny sharks called pups. Sharks grow slowly throughout their life. But many sharks die before they are fully grown. Most sharks do not live for more than 25 years.

Egg

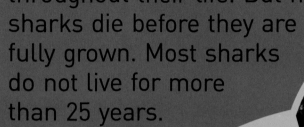

Young
swell shark

Adult
swell shark

Glossary

adapted an animal that has adapted has changed to suit the environment in which it lives

ampullae of Lorenzini tiny sensors near the front of a shark's head. These detect electrical signals produced when an animal moves

camouflage an animal's colouring that blends in with its background

filter feeder an animal that sieves, or removes, food such as small plants and animals from the water to eat

gills organs inside the body that are used to take in oxygen from water

gill slits slits, or gaps, where water passes out of the body

hatch to break out of an egg

invertebrate an animal without a backbone

overfishing taking too many fish from the ocean
pectoral fins fins that are positioned

just behind the gill slits

plankton tiny plants and animals that float in the upper layers of the ocean

predator an animal that hunts other animals

prey an animal that is hunted and eaten by other animals

shark finning the removal of fins from the body of a shark for use in soup

species a group of individuals that have the same appearance and are able to breed and produce young together

vibration a disturbance in the water caused by a moving object or animal

Index